What Managers Need to Stop Doing

Book 2 in the "Stop So You Can Get the Results

You Want" Series

BY

LIZ WEBER, CMC, CSP

Also by Liz Weber, CMC, CSP

Something Needs to Change Around Here: The Five Stages to Leveraging Your Leadership

Don't Let 'Em Treat You Like a Girl: A Woman's Guide to Leadership Success

What Business Owners Need to Stop Doing

What Human Resources Professionals Need to Stop Doing

What Women in Leadership Need to Stop Doing

Stop So You Can Get The Results You Want

Special Offer

If you enjoyed Liz's insights in this book, take advantage of these special offers:

1. Take Liz's Free Leadership Assessment to determine which of The Five Stages of Focused Leadership® you are currently modeling! Just go to her website, wbsllc.com, to access the assessment!

2. Click here to download Liz's white paper featuring the three things you need to stop today! Go to www.wbsllc.com/stop-it/

Social Media

Click on this link to visit my website:

http://www.WBSLLC.com

Or connect with me on social media:

LizWeberCMC

What Managers Need to Stop Doing

Book 2 in the "Stop So You Can Get the Results You Want" Series

By Liz Weber

Published 2019 by Aspen Hill Press

This book is dedicated to the thousands of managers who have attended my speeches and training programs. Your desire to continue to improve your management and leadership skills so you can better support your team members is inspiring and gratifying. I respect and appreciate you.

Liz

"Leadership is a series of behaviors

rather than a role for heroes."

Margaret Wheatley

Contents

Introduction

"A manager is a guide. He takes a group of people and says, 'with you, I can make us a success; I can show you the way.'"

— Arsène Wenger, manager, Arsenal Football Club

MANAGEMENT ISN'T EASY. In fact, many new managers are often shocked at the amount of work and responsibility expected of them. However, being a team leader, supervisor, or manager doesn't need to be as difficult as many cause it to be—not if you know what to stop doing.

The skills needed to be an effective manager are vastly different than those needed to be a proficient doer. Doers are the front-line, hands-on, do-the-work people. They're usually responsible for their individual output and for their specific, defined responsibilities. Proficient doers help create and then utilize systems and processes to help them do their jobs, but they still do the work themselves.

Effective managers, on the other hand, use the systems and processes to leverage and coordinate the work of many doers and thereby enhance the individual team member and unified team efforts.

They don't do the work their team members are being paid to do. Instead, effective managers ensure the systems and processes support the doers in doing their work.

Managers also are responsible for ensuring the work of the various doers is getting done on time, within budget, and in accordance with quality and customer specifications. Managers drive productivity and efficiency. Managers are responsible for ensuring the team members and the organization's resources (i.e., materials, facilities, money, etc.) are being utilized most effectively, here and now, to meet the organization's near-term goals and objectives.

However, managers often incorrectly believe their jobs are, in fact, to do the specific, itemized tasks listed in their position descriptions or on their work orders or on other project lists. Yes, those tasks need to get done. But those tasks are *expected*. Those are *the basics*. Those are the *bare minimum* requirements managers are expected to be able to do—and do well. That's what they're being paid to do.

Unfortunately, what most new or less-than-effective managers *don't* realize is what the leadership team *really* expects of them, because it's often not communicated well or at all. The leadership team really wants the managers to be accountable for and to take *ownership* of the problems, confusion, frustrations, and other issues their teams face that cause delays or roadblocks in their ability to get their work done. Being accountable and taking ownership doesn't mean taking all of the blame personally. It means taking the individual responsibility and initiative to identify, address, and clear the roadblocks the team is facing, struggling with, over-analyzing, under-analyzing, over-emphasizing, exaggerating, or completely missing. Whatever the issue is that's creating a roadblock to the team's successful performance, it's the manager's responsibility to clear it.

However, the manager needs to clear the issue in a way that isn't mean, but in a way that's "managed." So if the issue is one poor performer dragging the entire team down, the manager needs to address the poor performance issue. If the issue is interpersonal conflicts among team members, the manager needs to address the conflicts. If the issue is faulty equipment, unequal work distribution, or production challenges, the manager needs to address the faulty equipment, imbalance, and challenges head-on. Whatever the issue, the manager's job is to address it in a way that isn't mean, but in a way that's intentional and managed.

To be an effective manager, first, be accountable and take ownership of your management responsibilities and do so in a way that's managed, not mean.

Take ownership of your management responsibilities and do so in a way that's managed, not mean.

Second, learn to comfortably hold your team members accountable for their performance and behavior. Holding employees accountable doesn't need to become a conflict or argument; it just needs to be an upfront, clear, focused conversation. Prepare for a conversation not a conflict. Prepare for a conversation to ensure your employees are completely clear on how they are performing or behaving incorrectly and what they need to do to correct it.

Prepare for a conversation not a conflict.

Managing others is not easy and that's why I've compiled these two and eight other ideas in this book. I share my insights to help you identify what you may need to stop doing so you can become an even better, more effective manager. Some of the ideas shared here have been previously presented in some of my other writings, but they've been updated and organized here to serve as a roadmap for you and to help you become the manager your team needs you to be. Thank you for caring about your employees and your impact as their manager.

{ 1 } Stop Thinking "Managing" is Being "Mean"

"A leader leads by example not by force."

— Sun Tzu, author, The Art of War

WHY: IF YOU do your job well as a manager, there is no need to be mean. However, there is a need to be consistent in your behaviors and clear in your communications. If you do your job well as a manager, your team members will know what is expected of them. They will know you will support them. They will know you will hold them accountable if they are unable to—or choose not to—do what is expected of them to perform their jobs satisfactorily. If you do your job well as a manager, you will have created an environment and relationship with your team built on consistency and trust. They will trust you to do what you say, and you will trust them to be productive team members.

If you do your job well as a manager, there is no need to be mean.

To establish this relationship of consistency and trust, from my experience, the best managers rely on honest communications with their team members. As such, one of the nicest things managers can do for their employees is to give them a "heads-up" when an employee or employees are starting to behave in ways that are undesirable. The best managers are the ones who openly, honestly, and frequently keep employees clear and informed on what they're doing well, what needs to stop, and what needs to be enhanced.

That's not being mean. That's being transparent. That's being honest. That's being a manager. What's mean is NOT telling your employees when they are messing up. Trying to be nice by not immediately bringing concerns to your employees' attention is poor management. And let's be honest, it's also cowardly.

Over the years, I've seen many new as well as experienced managers equate being mean with being honest and being nice with not saying anything at all. For many, simply talking with their team members is difficult and stressful. When I hear of situations such as this, I ask myself:

Why is it so hard for so many managers to simply talk with their employees about less-than-expected performance?

Why do so many managers become mean when they simply need to make their employees aware their behaviors are taking them down the path towards disciplinary actions or worse—termination?

Why do so many managers default to "attack mode" instead of "talk mode" when they simply need to make employees aware of specific issues to correct?

From my experience, there are two common reasons for these behaviors. The first reason is that managers tend to model "disciplinary" behaviors they've seen or experienced themselves. They model snarky, sneaky (i.e., passive-aggressive), or just plain mean behaviors in attacking, belittling, and demeaning the employees who have frustrated them. They equate letting employees know they're performing in unacceptable ways with slamming the employees. They take a sledgehammer approach instead of a highlighter approach to make the employees aware the employees' performance is not acceptable. The managers attack in a big way instead of teach with insight.

Don't attack. Teach with insight.

The second most common reason for the attack mode is: Fear. Fear of having a "difficult conversation" with an employee. From my experience, managers often anticipate potentially, emotion-filled interactions that may result in hostility, tears, yelling, or hurt feelings. So, to "gear up" for such interactions, many managers put on their "attack gear." They get themselves worked up emotionally and mentally. The managers delay meeting with their employees until they have several examples of poor behavior so they can build a strong case against their employees.

As they delay and build their cases, the managers' frustration levels increase because the employees continue to perform poorly. Then, with emotion, the managers attack with proof instead of teach with small, incremental conversations along the way.

Gail had been a manager for years. Through her attention to detail, deadlines, and accuracy, Gail had gained the respect of many and had earned a reputation as a manager who could deliver products on time and within budget. As a participant in the leadership training my company provided to Gail's company, she, along with all of the management team, participated in various individual assessments. These assessments included input from peers, superiors, staff, customers, and others on various management and leadership behaviors and skills.

When I shared with Gail the results of her initial assessment, she was stunned. She was angry. Her managerial and leadership capabilities had never been criticized before. Yet, the feedback from numerous respondents had reiterated a few key themes: *Working with Gail is all work and no play. Gail is unyielding. Gail is dictatorial. Gail doesn't talk with you; Gail talks at you. Gail doesn't coach you; Gail points out what you've been doing wrong, makes you feel stupid, and then reprimands you.*

As I finished sharing the major themes identified in her assessment, Gail looked at me as tears welled up in her eyes, "Liz, I'm just trying to be a good manager." Gail was embarrassed and she was hurt.

Our conversation continued to be a difficult one for her as she struggled with my recommendation that, as a first step, she simply start to talk with her staff individually and as a team on a regular basis. Gail's eyes actually twitched as she processed this concept when I first suggested it.

"I couldn't do that." *Gail objected.*

"Why?"

"Well, we just don't have time for that kind of thing."

Gail did not casually talk with her staff. She typically arrived early, left late, and worked through lunch. Gail intentionally kept all conversations work related so as not to intrude on anyone's privacy or appear to be getting too "chummy" with anyone. As a result, she knew little about her staff, and they thought she was distant, cold, and mean.

In a subsequent coaching conversation with Gail, it quickly became obvious: She never meant to be mean or to project a distant, cold persona. She'd simply tried to behave the way she thought an effective manager should behave: efficient, strict, and unemotional. That's what she'd experienced in her formative work years. From Gail's experience, managers gave orders and workers did what they were told. There was no need to socialize with staff. There was no need to babysit staff and help them through personal issues. That wasn't what managers did. Besides, no manager had ever taken a personal interest in her or supported her during personal challenges. Gail had had to learn how to scrape by and advance on her own. From her perspective, it had worked for her, so she thought it should work for her staff too.

However, over several months, given the feedback she received from the assessments and the interactions with her peers during the training sessions, Gail's perspective on managing started to change. By experiencing for herself, the power of just talking with someone else about staff perceptions, as well as talking with her peers during training, Gail started to intentionally relax and talk with staff. She started to hold a team lunch, once a week, just to gather as a team during lunch and talk about whatever came up—work or personal issues. She made it a point to tell her team, "This isn't work time; it's lunch time."

As Gail later shared with me:

"At first, I could tell the team really didn't know what was going on. However, I've got a few people on the team who jumped at the chance to have a team lunch so they carried the conversation the first few times. By about the third or fourth week, I have to admit, I could tell I was loosening up and so was the team. It's not been easy and it's not been smooth. But now these lunches are something we all look forward to. I've learned a lot about my staff because of them, and

I believe they're getting to understand me better too.

I'm also more comfortable talking with staff right away when I see things they're doing wrong. I no longer wait until I have a few examples to share with them to prove my point. I just focus on making them aware of the mistakes so they can fix them, quickly.

I still have very high standards and my team knows that. In fact, I've had to let one staff member go. However, we've been doing this long enough now, that the rest of the team can joke about our work and the standards we have to meet right in front of me and they know I'll laugh along with them. They know the expectations and they *know the consequences if they don't meet them.*

They respect me and my position. But now I think

they're starting to realize I'm not trying to trick

them. They're no longer afraid to let me know

what they don't know, and I guess I no longer hold

it against them. I'm trying to just focus on helping

them find ways to get the work done."

Nicely done Gail. That's what an effective manager does.

Here's what I suggest you do instead: Your job as a manager is to get things done working through your staff. For that to happen, you need to be clear on what is expected of them, when, and how. You don't need to be a dictator, but you don't need to be their friend either; you need to be fair, be consistent, and be a clear communicator. This is simple to say, but hard for many managers to do.

You don't need to be a dictator, but you don't need to be their friend either; you need to be fair, be consistent, and be a clear communicator.

Create a forum for you and your team to be honest with each other so that all of you can stay on track. If you don't hold regular team meetings, do it. If you haven't yet created team rules or values—do so. If you have them—use them. If you don't connect on a regular basis as a team just to spend time together, do it. Dedicate time to learn how to comfortably interact and communicate with each other.

If you are an effective manager, there is no need to be mean because you will have created an environment where your team members are constantly allowed to make an important choice: to either continue to be a part of your team, or not. If they want to be a part of your team, they know you will support them, but you will also hold them accountable to do the jobs they're being paid to do. If they don't want to continue to be a part of your team, that's OK too.

Be comfortable being a strong manager. Keep in mind: Strong managers are fair. They are transparent. They clue employees in when they're doing things well and they clue employees in when they're starting to veer off-track. They make employees aware when they appreciate their work, and they make employees aware of their concerns. They address inappropriate behaviors and under-performance immediately. Strong, effective managers create a culture of trust and enable choices. Mean managers don't.

"The challenge of leadership is to be strong, but not rude; be kind, but not weak; be bold, but not bully; ...be proud, but not arrogant; have humor, but without folly."

—   *Jim Rohn, author and leadership expert*

{ 2 } Stop Trying to Be Their Friend and Also Their Manager

"When we fail to set boundaries and hold

people accountable, we feel used and

mistreated."

— *Brené Brown, author, The Gifts of*

Imperfection: Let Go of Who You Think You're

Supposed to Be and Embrace Who You Are

WHY: IT'S NOT your job to be their friend. It's

your job to be their manager. In those instances

where you were, in fact, their peer or friend before

you became their manager, it's confusing for you and them if you continue to behave as their friend in your role as their manager. Besides, more often than not, you're not their friend. You've just become friendly with them as your working relationship has evolved.

When you are promoted to managing your friends and former peers, it's hard. You may have some team members now who do not take you seriously in your new role, or some may resent you because they too had wanted the manager's position. Either way, it's an uncomfortable situation until you clarify your role and theirs.

It's not your job to be their friend. It's your job to be their manager.

Adyn was not only the youngest member of his team, he'd also just been promoted to being the manager. Of the nine people he now supervised, two had applied for the manager's position, and the other seven had been there longer than Adyn. As he shared with me, *"They're not openly hostile to me, but I can sense they resent having to report to me now. I've tried to give them as much leeway as I can, but I'm going to have to do something soon or I don't think they're ever going to respect me in this position."*

In talking with Adyn further, he shared that he had not yet had a full team meeting since his promotion. Given that, I suggested he pull everyone together to openly discuss the reality of his promotion. Let the team know he is keenly aware others had also wanted the position, but the position had been given to him and he now has the obligation to fulfill it.

I suggested Adyn also clarify the team's near and longer-term goals being tracked by management, how he would be supporting them going forward, and what he needed of each of them in their roles to successfully move things forward. The conversation would serve several purposes: 1) Create a format for future, relaxed but informative team meetings (something previous managers had not done), 2) Establish his role as the manager and overtly state his anticipated behavior as such, and 3) Clarify what his expectations of each team member's role and responsibilities were going forward. Adyn needed to clarify his expectation for himself: He would be supportive of them, but it was his job to be the manager. The fact that he happened to manage his *former* peers, was secondary.

For many, having established friendly relationships with staff also poses problems. Several years ago, as I was starting a day-long management training program, I asked the participants what specific management issues they would like me to address. One manager, Brenda, raised her hand and said, "I'd like to learn how to provide feedback to my staff without changing our relationship."

Well this was an interesting request, so I asked Brenda to elaborate what she meant by "without changing our relationship."

"You see," she explained, "I get along really well with everyone on my team. I've got a great group of people working with me and I like every one of them. I just don't think they work as hard as they could. I think they could perform better. "

Wow. This was an incredible insight. Brenda had obviously established a friendly relationship with her team. However, she was not effectively managing them. In my straightforward way, I asked, "Brenda think about this for a minute: If your relationship with your staff is so great, why aren't they doing what you need them to do and why don't they know you're not satisfied with their current level of performance?"

Brenda looked at me in stunned silence for a few seconds. Then she simply nodded and said, "OK, I get your point."

Jonah had also intentionally tried to be a "friendly" manager. He had been a manager for over 20 years and had typically managed staff his same age or older. Due to a job change, Jonah was now managing Shenise, a new team member who was only slightly older than his college-aged daughters. So as not to appear overly strict and parental, Jonah had intentionally created a relaxed, informal relationship with her. Yet, he was frustrated by her performance.

There was no doubt Shenise was smart. She'd come highly recommended and quickly understood the many complex issues their office addressed. However, Shenise consistently missed deadlines, failed to provide regular project updates, and tended to adjust her project task list without input or approval by Jonah. Jonah shared his frustration:

"I made it very clear, the reports were due at the end of May. But don't you know, May came and went. No reports. June came and went. No

reports. Now we're almost to the end of July, and I still haven't seen them. I don't know what Shenise is thinking but I never would have treated my boss this way. I'm trying to be patient with her, but she doesn't seem to pick up on my clues."

Clues? "What clues?" I asked Jonah.

"Well, when she walks by my office, I'll tap the pile of project reports I'm reviewing from the other team members, thinking she'll get the hint."

"Jonah, why are you hinting? Why are you trying to send her clues? Treat her like an adult. Talk with her as you would any other team member. Tell her, very clearly, what needs to change, what needs to be done and by when. Stop hinting. Start talking."

Stop hinting. Start talking.

Jonah had thought that by hinting instead of directly telling Shenise what he needed her to do, he was mentoring her. He didn't believe that he could be a good mentor if she perceived him as coming down hard on her. However his hints weren't being picked up; therefore, he was unintentionally condoning her behavior and training her to ignore the stated deadlines. His responsibility to her as her manager was to be fair and clear.

"Jonah, tapping a pile of files can be misinterpreted in numerous ways. Saying,

'Shenise, the reports need to be completed by close of business Thursday,' cannot."

"OK. I get your point."

My point with both Brenda and Jonah was simply this: If your staff isn't doing what you want and need them to do, ask yourself: Why? Why aren't they performing to the level I want and need?

- Have I made my expectations clear and not open to interpretation?
- Am I providing regular feedback on what they're doing well and what needs to change?

- Have I allowed myself to become frustrated with my team because I have tried to be nice by not being honest with them?

Both Brenda and Jonah were afraid the relaxed, friendly relationships they'd created would change if they made their respective team members aware their performance wasn't where it needed to be. However, as I outlined in Chapter 1, one of the nicest things you can do as a manager is to let your team members know when they're messing up before things go too far. The longer you say nothing, the longer you condone their less-than-acceptable performance, and the more frustrated you (and other team members) become. Don't wait until you're past being just frustrated, and you've become angry. Say something. Do something.

Look at it this way, wouldn't you appreciate a friend telling you that you have a piece of spinach stuck between your front teeth instead of letting you walk around like that? You'd appreciate your friend bringing that embarrassing issue to your attention so you can correct it, right? If instead, your friend didn't tell you and let you walk around all day with spinach in your teeth, but later said something like, "I didn't feel comfortable telling you because I didn't want to embarrass you." You'd probably be angry with your friend for not having the courage to speak up to make you aware of the situation so you could fix it quickly.

I shared the above analogy with Jonah. With a few more words of encouragement and advice on how to have a Necessary Conversation, Jonah talked with Shenise and clarified his expectations. Shenise was surprised when Jonah explained his relaxed manner didn't translate to relaxed deadlines. Shenise was rightly somewhat frustrated that Jonah hadn't talked with her sooner, but she now understood and started to meet deadlines and other expectations with more regularity. As Jonah's management became clearer, Shenise's performance improved.

Here's what I suggest you do instead: The sooner you address issues and conflicts, the sooner they are resolved. The more frequent your interactions and communications with your staff are, the more comfortable they will be with your comments—positive and negative. The longer you delay, minor issues often become bigger issues than they need to be, and if you only communicate to point out mistakes, your team members rightly view your feedback as criticisms not insights.

If you are, indeed friends with your team members and socialize with them outside of work, it's critical to your relationship that you clarify your management role at work versus your friend role outside work.

Keep in mind, it's not your job to be their friend. It's your job to be their manager. So don't expect to make many friends in the workplace or to keep the same relationships with your co-worker friends as you enter a managerial role. You can be friendly; it's just hard to truly be friends. Also, as you move up in the hierarchy of an organization, you have to take on more and more responsibilities and you'll need to make decisions quicker and quicker. The sheer magnitude of the issues you'll have to deal with on an hourly, much less daily basis, will prohibit you from being able to project the same collegial characteristics you shared readily and regularly before. It's not that you don't care anymore. It's just that you have numerous other issues weighing on you now, and many of them cannot be shared with your former peers.

I've shared this idea in other writings, but I'll share it again because I've seen it work with many of my clients. If you do nothing else, stop thinking of conversations with your employees about their poor performance as "difficult conversations." That term alone brings to mind the anxiety and negative emotions outlined above. Instead, think of conversations you need to have with your employees about their poor performance as "Necessary Conversations™." They're necessary because you need to clue your employees in now. They're necessary because if they don't occur, your employees are likely to continue down an unacceptable path of behavior. They're necessary because it's part of your job to teach, inform, refocus, and guide your employees—not slam them. These conversations are necessary because they'll help you talk with your employees instead of attack your employees.

Here is my **Ten Step Process for Having Necessary Conversations™**:

1. Determine if this is a one-time event or if a trend is emerging. *(If the team member comes* *to you and says, "I just made a mistake!" and then describes what she did wrong. There's no need for a conversation. She knows she performed in a less-than-desired way. However if you become aware of an inappropriate or behavior that's veering off-track you should immediately have a conversation with her. If you didn't address it the first time you became aware of the behavior and you see it again, you must address it. Occurring once could have been an accident or flook on her part. Occurring twice is a trend and you need to make her aware of the issue. Keep this positioned as a conversation not a reprimand. Your purpose is to make your team member aware of an unacceptable behavior they may not be aware of.*

You do not want to have to escalate this to a disciplinary action.)

2. Identify the employee's personality and communication style. *(This helps you communicate in a way your team member will easily relate to and not shut down on you. You want her to relax and listen to what you have to share.)*

3. State the *specific* behavior that's unacceptable. *(Be specific and clear. Don't generalize and say something such as, "You have a bad attitude." That's open to interpretation. That could mean she is uncooperative, or grumpy,* *or combative. State specifically what she is doing that is unacceptable. "Denise, you may not be aware, but when Koda shares her ideas in our team meetings, you roll your eyes." That's specific and Denise knows exactly what you're talking about. It may well sound petty to her, but you want her to see in her mind's eye the specific behavior that needs to change.)*

4. Explain why it matters and why you are making them aware. *(Just as this step indicates, its purpose is to help your Denise understand why you're raising this issue with her. "I'm raising this with you because it's disrespectful to Koda. She sees it. The other team members also see it, and* *it's causing them to shut down. I need every team member to be able to comfortably share ideas without being disrespected and fear of judgement. That type of environment enables us to be successful.)*

5. Ask for input or an explanation and look at them and wait. *(This step is where you ask Denise to help you understand her behavior. However, after you ask the question, look at her and wait for a response. By just asking the question and then looking at Denise for an answer, you'll cause her to start to take ownership of the behavior. It also helps you uncover issues you may not be aware of. Ask Denise, "Why do* *you do roll your eyes when Koda shares information?" and then look at her calmly but directly. You may have to quietly look at her for 3-5 seconds until she says something)*

6. Ask for an action-oriented solution – the team member needs to 'own'. *(Again, you're looking to your team member to 'own' her behavior and also 'own' her solution. Simply look at Denise and ask, "What will you do to correct this?" and again calmly wait 3-5 seconds for a response.)* **If the solution provided is acceptable—go to step 7. If not, you provide a solution.** *("I'm sure you are joking, but telling them to 'Grow up and deal with it' is not the* *solution Denise. So, here's what I need you to do: You need to immediately stop rolling your eyes whenever Koda shares an idea or comment you don't like. When you disagree, wait your turn in the que to share your concern or alternative idea.")*

7. Recap the solution and clarify the consequences for non-performance. *(This step is critical because this is where you clarify for your team member that she will own the action **you** take next. Be specific and clear. This is not a threat. This is a clarification of choices: Either Denise corrects her behavior and this issue is considered resolved, or you will take further* *action. "OK. Let me recap and clarify where we are. You will immediately stop rolling your eyes whenever Koda shares an idea or comment you don't like. If, however, that behavior continues, Denise, I will have another conversation with you and that conversation will start the official disciplinary process.)*

8. Ask a closed question to prompt agreement. *(This is nice way to ask your team member to support your request. "Denise, can I count on you to take care of this?")*

9. Schedule a follow-up conversation. *(If the issue is important enough for you to talk with the* employee about it in the first place, it's important enough to follow-up on. *"Denise, let's meet briefly after next week's team meeting to review how we'll progress."*)

10. Follow up. *(Again, if this issue is important enough to discuss, follow up and close this conversation circle. This follow-up doesn't need to be extensive. It can be a 10-second comment in the hallway. But let the employee know you've tracked this behavior to a "close". "Denise, thank you for not rolling your eyes today and for interacting with the others more collaboratively. I appreciate it. It made a* *difference in today's meeting. Let's keep this going.")*

To help you prepare for a conversation and not an argument, here are some tips for keeping Necessary Conversations™ focused and as free of conflict and hostility as possible:

Be crystal clear about the subject of your conversation with your employees.

You will be addressing a fact: unacceptable behavior or performance. You will also be clarifying with them a resolution. That's the point of the conversation. It's not to debate perspectives.

Don't let the potential reactions you may or may not be confronted with stop you or impact what you share.

Don't get yourself worked up dreading how the employee may or may not react. Don't prepare for a conflict. Prepare for a conversation and keep yourself and them focused on the issues (i.e., unacceptable performance) and the desired outcome (i.e., a clarity that they will be in control of choosing which way future conversations and actions go: Either they change their behavior or they will choose the consequences).

Don't let hurt feelings, anger, or hostility sidetrack you.

Keep in mind, your intent is to be fair, honest and professional. You are trying to be as transparent as possible by treating your team members as adults who are capable of making choices concerning their future. If an employee responds with anger, tears, or complete shock, reiterate your purpose for having this conversation: "I don't mean to hurt your feelings. I mean to be helpful. I want you to be aware of these issues so you have a choice and a chance in correcting them before I need to take any further action."

If you do your job well as a manager and clearly and consistently communicate with your team, they'll always know where they stand with you. They won't view you as their friend. They'll view you as their manager, who they trust and respect.

"It takes a great deal of bravery to stand up to our enemies, but just as much to stand up to our friends."

— *J.K. Rowling, author, Harry Potter series*

{ 3 } Stop Complaining About the Team You Inherited

"Be a strong leader, even if you follow a

weak leader."

— *Miles Anthony Smith, author, Why*

Leadership Sucks

WHY: YOUR TEAM is *your* team; it doesn't really matter how you came together, but it does matter how you manage your team going forward.

Sadly, taking over a team from a less-than-effective manager is not uncommon. In fact, I see it frequently. My company provides a quarterly training program for a large government agency to help its new managers address conflict and difficult employee behaviors more effectively. Without fail, each class has several managers who are new to the agency or who have been promoted from peer to manager. Their most desired take-away from the day of training is: "How do I deal with the team I inherited? The previous manager didn't address performance issues, and now I'm stuck with a team that thinks showing up is good enough."

Karen was a participant in one of these training sessions. She had been promoted four months earlier and had inherited the team from Josh. He was a nice man, but he was an ineffective manager. Josh thought being "nice" meant not holding team members accountable to do their jobs. So he didn't.

Like many conflict-averse managers, Josh found it easier to simply ignore select team members' clearly unacceptable behaviors and performance. When tasks were not getting done by challenging team members, Josh would delegate the tasks to someone else or he would do them himself. He preferred to shift the burden to others or do the work himself, instead of addressing the issues with the poorly performing team members.

As a result, Josh had created a team that did not know how or want to work together. Josh's lax management style had created rifts, tension, dysfunction, and uneven workloads within the team. The poor performers' behaviors had been reinforced because they were allowed, and the strong performers were resentful because they were expected to do the bulk of the work. Needless to say, Karen now was responsible for team members that didn't like one another, much less know how to work well together, and they didn't much care for her either.

Karen's first several months as the manager were difficult. Karen had clarified their performance expectations where they had been ignored before. She had held regular team meetings, yet they weren't helping the team connect or work any better together. With a deep sigh, Karen said, "I never seem to make progress. When I attack one personnel issue, I have staff run to me to tell me about several more. And, I have other staff members that seem to thrive on trying to sabotage any progress I make. When is this going to end?"

At this point, Karen could have followed Josh's lead and ignored the headaches caused by the more challenging, inherited team members.

She could have become a wimpy manager. She could have done the "easy" thing and simply focused her energies on supporting the more cooperative team members. Luckily for her, the team she inherited, and the agency, she didn't.

Your team is your team; it doesn't matter how you came together, but it does matter how you manage your team going forward.

Here's what I suggest you do instead: Don't focus on what did or did not happen under the previous management. If you inherited a less-than-effective team, obviously prior management could have done things differently, but didn't. The main point is, don't do the same thing. Don't be a wimpy manager because you're afraid of conflict or of taking on challenging issues.

Dealing with difficult issues and confronting conflicts *is* a large part of your job as a manager. So if a challenging issue your team faces is working with one or more difficult team members who should be replaced by members who will be a better long-term fit for your organization, start the process to make the changes. If the challenge is select staff not doing work they should have been doing for months if not years, teach them what to do and then hold them accountable. If the conflict is between team members and their perception of inequitable workloads, address the perception or the reality of the imbalance.

As the manager, your job is to create a work environment that your team members can work in comfortably. They need to be able to focus on their work and do the jobs they're being paid to do. So whatever you, as the manager, need to do to resolve issues that are preventing that from happening, you need to do it. That's your job.

As the manager, you need to resolve issues that are preventing your team members' ability to focus on their work and do the jobs they're being paid to do.

That's your job.

After hearing about Karen's difficulties with her team, she and I spoke about being a leader and a manager. She knew what her job and responsibilities were. She knew it would be hard. However, she hadn't anticipated the level of resistance she would face from her team, many of whom she'd known before she took the position.

To help her, Karen and I talked about the process for changing a team's culture and the time it would take. We briefly identified a rough timeline with select actions she would take and identified a handful of non-negotiable changes she needed to see with select team members—or she would initiate the termination process as needed (i.e. something not experienced by the team in the past 15+ years.) But first, Karen would hold a team meeting to recalibrate their starting point as a team, restate her role and expectations of herself, address their expectations of her, clarify with them their roles and her expectations of them, and outline how she would support them or address unacceptable issues going forward. There would be no surprises. Karen would be honest and fair in letting her team know she wasn't going to ignore the tsunami of issues that faced them. She would work through the issues with them to create a more functional team, one issue at a time.

One year later, Karen approached me after a keynote speech I gave at a state-wide event. She shared, that finally, after one year, her team had "turned the corner." As we had planned, she'd held the first of many meetings with her entire team. She had clarified everyone's role, responsibilities, their shared mission, and her willingness to enforce consequences for non-performance. As she consistently repeated the same message and followed through on what she said she would do, her team started to believe her, trust her, and things started to change.

A few of the underperformers enhanced their performance. One transferred to a different office, and she had had to replace two team members. Her strong team members thanked her for supporting them, for holding people accountable, and for creating a more equitable, professional, and collaborative workplace. Even though Karen had inherited most of her team members and could have continued to blame others, she didn't. She did her job.

"If you could kick the person in the pants

responsible for most of your trouble, you

wouldn't sit for a month."

— *Theodore Roosevelt, 26th President of*

the United States

{ 4 } Stop Confusing Your Team By Being Unclear Yourself

"You can have brilliant ideas, but if you can't get them across, your ideas won't get you anywhere."

— Lee Iacocca, former CEO, Chrysler Corporation

WHY: IF YOU don't know what you're talking about, how is your team supposed to know what you want?

Communicating clearly is one of the most important skills for any manager to have, yet it's one that many will roll their eyes at when they hear it's to be a topic of discussion or management training.

Who needs that touchy-feely crap? I know how to talk. The problem is nobody listens.

Yeah, well for communication to be effective, you need to ensure that what you are trying to communicate is being received and understood by others, and therefore it's your responsibility, as the manager, to not only "know how to talk" but to "know how to talk so others will listen and understand you." And that's where the screw-ups occur. For the most part, most managers have no problem talking. The problem is they talk in ways that make it difficult for others to listen to or understand them.

If you don't know what you're talking about, how is your team supposed to know what you want?

In working with my clients on strategic planning or leadership training, I see managers struggle with communicating clearly in numerous ways. Whether it's clarifying a needed behavioral change or outlining the company's next major strategy, too many managers trip over themselves and their word choice as they attempt to relay information to their teams.

For example, too many managers can't articulate how they want their employees' performance to improve. They just want it to "get better." Too many managers can't articulate what their employees need to do to work better together. The employees just need to "get better attitudes." The managers may visualize what they want, but without articulating the specific desired behavior changes clearly, they cause the employees to interpret and guess—and that typically doesn't result in what the managers want. Without being specific in their word choice, the managers are causing guesses, confusion, and frustration.

Similarly, when managers use specific words, but in the wrong way, they also cause confusion and frustration.

On a recent return flight from a speaking engagement, I started talking with the gentleman sitting next to me. Roger was a senior level manager for a 250-employee defense contractor and was traveling to meet with the rest of his company's leadership team for an off-site management and strategy meeting. Roger was finishing his notes on what he wanted to present to help create greater clarity, energy, and productivity throughout the employee population.

When I shared with Roger what my company did, he asked, "Would you mind taking a look at my notes and giving me a few pointers? This is the first time we've held an off-site leadership retreat since the new CEO came on board last year, so I'd like to make my points as solid and clear as possible."

Absolutely!

As I read through Roger's ideas, his intent was solid. His passion for helping the employees was clear. His acknowledgement of current and prior management missteps and failures was honest and bare. However, Roger's plan for improvements was flawed by a common management mistake: Roger wasn't using the right terms consistently to enhance clarity, consistency, and action. It became quickly evident Roger really didn't know the strategic planning terms he was using.

He was making the same mistake many in management make: They believe they know how to use the terms because they've heard them so many times before. However, because they've not really used them as a management and leadership tool before, they don't use the terms correctly. As a result, like many other managers, Roger was setting himself and the leadership team up for embarrassment, confusion, mixed messaging, and frustration.

Here are some of the concepts managers are often told to communicate to their teams, and how

Roger proposed to communicate them with his leadership peers:

Vision: Roger had outlined the very real need to clarify the company's vision for the employees. The employees needed to know what the leadership team expected. That's true and important. However, Roger's company doesn't have a clear vision. Instead they've historically focused on "winning contracts." To provide clarity, Roger outlined their vision as: *Win Contracts; Double in Size; Implement Well; Strive to be the Respected Industry Leader; Integrity; Teamwork; Profitability.* Those are nice ideas, but Roger just blurred goals with values. A vision is the big goal your organization is trying to achieve; how you behave are your values. Roger had, in fact, suggested a vision: *Double in Size*, but he had buried it among everything else.

Mission: The mission statement Roger included in his notes had been developed years before and was clear and without fluff. In one sentence, it outlined broadly what his company did; why it existed. Perfect.

Values: Roger's company didn't have values specified. However, as noted above, he had included some basic expected behaviors (i.e., values) in his proposed vision. I explained to Roger, that he should suggest the leadership team draft an initial set of behaviors (i.e., values) expected of everyone to help them and all the employees move towards their vision. Things such as: *Share Knowledge, Take Risks Wisely, Communicate Clearly and Often, Take Ownership of Problems, Consider the Big Picture Impact*, etc. are sample values that he and his peers could consider, as these behaviors would cause employees to think, learn, share, and grow—all of which align with an organization that wants to grow.

Strategic Objectives: Roger had listed strategic objectives he believed the company needed to pursue, yet, like many managers when outlining outcomes, the list Roger had created was a mix of organizational development changes needed, R&D actions, numerous tactical administrative actions, and a few long-term goals. When I asked Roger to clarify the difference between strategic objectives and goals, he looked at me, opened his mouth, closed his mouth, and then said, *"I don't know."*

Strategic objectives are big picture themes of WHAT you want to accomplish going forward. So, ideas such as: Improve Employee Engagement, Increase R&D Production, Reduce

Waste and Inefficiencies are big picture ideas of what you are going to do to move towards your vision. To implement them, you need specific actions to clarify HOW you're going to them. You need goals.

Goals: Strategic Goals are the big chunky projects your organization needs to take on (over and above current operations) to move your organization towards your vision. Goals have due dates, specific deliverables, and are comprised of numerous sub-goals and projects. The sub-goals and projects are what are divvied out to staff to help move things forward.

Roger had great ideas. He simply had the wrong words.

Most managers have no problem talking. The problem is they talk in ways that make it difficult for others to listen or to understand them.

Here's what I suggest you do instead: Be as clear and intentional in your communication as you can. Until your team knows you so well they can identify your true meaning without your needing to say much, you need to ensure your communication is consistent, clear, and not open to interpretation. You also need to know what to say, when to talk—and when to stop.

Managers know they're supposed to communicate, communicate, communicate. In fact, managers are often told to "over-communicate." That's great advice—in general. However, where many managers run amuck, is they confuse over-communicating with talking too much.

Many managers run amuck when they confuse over-communicating with talking too much.

Over-communicating simply means you communicate the same, clear, concise message over and over again so every employee who needs to hear it and understand it—does. In fact, when you "over-communicate" clearly and well, your employees know the message, can recite the message, and probably dream about the message because they've heard it so many times. However, as a result, there is no confusion in any one's mind what the vision is, what the goals are, what your expectations are, or whatever it is you have been communicating clearly and consistently. As a result, everyone is positioned to support the same message.

Talking too much, on the other hand, is simply using too many words, in too many various ways, to try to convey your message. When you talk too much, you often:

- Overwhelm your employees with too much information
- Confuse your employees with the variety of words, definitions, and messages you shared
- Create chaos as every employee will interpret your message differently and therefore pursue different objectives

- Bore your employees with all of your blah, blah, blah, so they simply tune you out.

If you believe or know you need to communicate more with your employees, congratulations. That's one step towards stronger leadership. However, before you start communicating, communicating, communicating, determine clearly what it is you need your employees to hear and understand. Then determine: What is the most basic, clear way to communicate that idea to my employees to minimize confusion?

As I walked Roger through the terms he had included in his talking points, how to use them properly, and how to tighten up his presentation, his eyes lit up.

"Thanks. That could have been really confusing to everyone and I wouldn't have been able to defend or clarify my ideas. You really do need to know what you're talking about to be an effective leader."

Yes you do.

"If you can't explain it simply, you don't understand it well enough."

— Albert Einstein, theoretical physicist

{ 5 } Stop Lying On Performance Reviews

"Even your most talented employees have room for growth in some area, and you're doing your employee a disservice if the sum of your review is, 'you're great!'"

— Kathryn Minshew, co-founder and CEO of The Muse

WHY: YOU'RE LYING. Sooner or later, the truth will come out that you've been exaggerating one or more team members' performance and you'll have to explain why. Also, by lying to your team members as to their true level of performance, you're setting yourself and them up for confused expectations going forward. Being honest now can save you a whole lot of trouble later!

When you exaggerate performance, from my observations, it's typically done for one of two reasons: 1) You're tolerating (and therefore rewarding) your team member's poor performance, so you can avoid an uncomfortable conversation with him or her, or 2) You don't want to "hurt anyone's feelings" by stating honestly that the employee's performance is "Satisfactory". It's not great nor is it poor. They're doing what is necessary to perform their job—no more and no less.

But since no one likes to be *just* "Acceptable" or "Satisfactory," you pump up your team members' ratings to "Exceptional" so they can feel good about themselves. Your attempts to be nice and spare your team's feelings by lying on their performance reviews are only hurting you and them.

When you don't honestly rate poor behavior by just one team member or your whole team, you are, by default, condoning their behavior and also rewarding them for it. So what's their incentive to change? There is none. When you rate less-than-desired performance as "Acceptable" or

"Exceptional," you've just rewarded your employees for their current mode of behavior, so why should they change? You've also created a confused reality for them. When you rate their satisfactory performance as "Exceptional," why are you frustrated with them and their performance? Is nothing ever good enough for you?

When you don't honestly rate poor behavior, you are, in fact, condoning it.

Your team is your team, and it's your responsibility to be their manager. It's your responsibility to help them to grow in their positions and enhance their skills. It's your responsibility to ensure they're acceptably performing their current full scope of job responsibilities, while they prepare for new responsibilities that may require additional skills. So you need to help them constantly not only perform current job responsibilities well and consistently, but you also need to help them hone new skills. If their current level of performance isn't up-to-par, how will they ever be able to meet their increased skill needs? It's time to be honest with your employees about how they're really performing.

I don't like conversations about performance issues any more than any other manager. However, to be fair, honest, and transparent, the conversations need to occur. That's why I shared how to have Necessary Conversations™ in Chapter 2. Communicate calmly and clearly what your concern is, why there is a concern, and what needs to change. Ensure your team members are aware early so they have a chance and a choice in changing their behavior or performance.

Whatever your reasoning for not addressing poor performance, your job is to ensure the work gets done and that it's done correctly. Let's be honest, if a certain piece of equipment started to malfunction and churn out parts that were not up to standard, would you simply stand by and let it continue to spew defective parts? No. You would shut down the unit, determine the cause of the malfunction, and then fix it.

As the machine restarted, you would stand by the machine to monitor it to ensure the parts were being produced correctly again. You may even continue to interact with and tweak the machine until it operated the way you know it could and should. So why don't you do the same thing with your team? Be honest. Monitor and address their performance to ensure it's where it needs to be, and evaluate their performance for what it really is.

Similarly, if your team members are good workers and are doing just what is expected—that's great! However, that's what they're supposed to do in exchange for their paychecks. Doing what they were hired to do, on time, to meet the established standards... is expected. It's not "Exceptional." You can and should be grateful to your team members for coming in every day and doing good work. Thank them regularly for helping you and for working with you.

However, don't inflate their performance ratings to skew their perception of what is *expected* versus what is *exceptional*. When you interchange those ideas, your team members are rightly confused when you tell them they could improve. How or why should they improve if they're already doing exceptional work? What's their incentive? Are you going to pay them more? Typically not.

Be honest. Monitor and address their performance to ensure it's where it needs to be, and evaluate their performance for what it really is.

Barry was hired as the new Director of Operations, with the directive to improve operations, efficiencies, and performance. In his first several months, Barry shared that he'd spent a great deal of time getting to know his team members, complementing them on their work, thanking them for being part of the team, and acknowledging their expertise. However, as skilled, technically savvy, and professional as his team was in so many areas, there were a few who did only what was expected and had excuses as to why they couldn't do more, stay longer, or carry any more of the workload.

He said to me, "Liz, these guys are some of the best there are in the industry. It's demeaning to them if I minimize them and their expertise and only give an 'Acceptable' because of something like work hours." That may be true, but it's still not an acceptable reason to not be truthful with them.

If your employees aren't clear as to what your standards are, you're causing them to guess. Or, by default, you're allowing them to continue to under-perform or demonstrate behaviors that you believe are "inappropriate." You continue to be frustrated with them, and they continue to under-perform. This vicious cycle is your fault; it's not theirs.

The vicious cycle is your fault; it's not theirs.

Here's what I suggest you do instead: Treat your team members with the dignity and respect they deserve by telling them the truth about their performance early and often, and rate them honestly. As Ronald Katz says, "Your standards are not what you say, they're what you accept." Clarify what your expectations and standards are and how you will evaluate and rate their performance. Be clear. Be transparent. Then follow through.

Start talking with your team members now. Clarify that "Exceptional" is not simply doing what is expected. Exceptional performance is rare and clearly at such a level that it far exceeds what was expected. You'll need to re-educate and retrain your team not to expect consistent "Exceptional" ratings going forward. That's neither fair nor logical. Start recalibrating with them now what is considered "Unacceptable," "Acceptable," and "Exceptional" (or whatever your standards are) performance so they know how you will rate their performance going forward.

If you communicate your expectations clearly, and then evaluate accordingly, there should be no surprises. If at any time, your team members are surprised at how you've rated their performance, you've not communicated clearly enough. You *will have* succeeded in clarifying your expectations for performance if during future performance reviews, your team members see their ratings and basically say, "Ok. There's nothing new here. I've heard all this before."

If you communicate your expectations clearly, and then evaluate accordingly, there should be no surprises.

In helping Barry create a culture of "No Surprises!" I coached him in clarifying his expectations for all team members concerning not only technical performance, but work hours, workload, etc. Over the course of the next year, Barry gathered data on production, attendance, billable hours, overtime, etc. He kept his entire team and all team members informed and aware of what the standards were and which were being met and not met.

As a result, he also had data on who was working "hard" and who was "getting by." Six months before the official performance reviews would be conducted, Barry held another team meeting in which he communicated his "leadership line-in-the-sand" on work hours, overtime, production standards, etc. He also clearly stated he would ensure going forward the workload would be more evenly spread across all team members. As a result, the employees who were already working 20+ hours of overtime a week to meet the customers' needs, would obviously get relief as others would be required to help with the heavy workload. The few employees who had had attendance issues and had not been willing to perform to these clearly defined standards understood the ramifications of being on one side of Barry's leadership line or the other.

As Barry shared with me, he had a conversation with an underperforming employee that went like this:

"So I guess you want to ensure the work is more evenly distributed."

"Yep," replied Barry, *"That's right."*

"I agree it should be evenly distributed.... But that'll mean I'll have to work more."

"Yep."

"But I'll have to change my commuting schedule."

"Yep."

"But this is going to be more work for me!"

"Yep."

"So,... could I, like, lose my job if I don't work the additional hours?"

"Yep."

This may sound cold to some, but which side of the leadership line will the underperforming employee choose? Whichever side it is, it's his choice. Now that he knows where the line is, he can choose. And however he chooses, that's how he'll be evaluated. He'll be told the truth. He won't be surprised.

To minimize anxiety and the potential for surprises with performance reviews, create a more honest and effective performance management culture. Try these steps:

1. Earn your team's trust and respect *(Note: This won't happen overnight).*

It's pretty tough for a manager to critique an employee's performance and have his or her comments be well-received when there's little to no trust or respect between the manager and the employee. Trust and respect take time to earn. Start to build that type of relationship now so your entire team knows and trusts you to regularly share what's working and what's not. Build that type of relationship with your team, and there will be no surprises.

2. Determine and communicate clear expectations and job duties.

Communicate clearly and regularly your organization's values so there is no guessing as to what behaviors you expect of everyone day in and day out. Also, review and share with every new hire and current employee a basic listing of what the person filling that position is expected to do on a daily, weekly, monthly, quarterly, and annual basis. The list of what they need to be able to do—specifically—needs to be clear to both you and them so no one has to guess.

3. Determine and communicate the performance standards.

Once it's clear what the employee is supposed to do, it also needs to be made clear to what standard the work is to be done. If the performance rating scale has "Exceptional" as its highest rating, the employee needs to be told what "Exceptional" performance looks like, so he or she knows the standard you will use in the rating process. If you can't clarify what "Exceptional" performance is or what it looks like, how are your team members supposed to know how to perform to "Exceptional" standards? You need to be clear on this yourself so you can clarify your standards to your team.

4. Communicate and document job performance all year long.

I've shared it several times already, but if you do your job right, there should be no surprises at review time. There should be nothing new your employees haven't heard and have had a chance to address before, However, too often, all the formal performance review meeting is, is a rehashing of all the things done wrong all year long that were never addressed when they occurred. When an employee does something wrong or is starting to exhibit behaviors that are not acceptable, have the Necessary Conversations™. Make sure the employee knows what s/he is doing is wrong—and be specific. Specify what is not acceptable. Make the employee aware of the behavior or performance that is not acceptable, help identify how to correct it, and then follow up.

Document the conversation, not as a reprimand but as a journaled item to track and note performance changes or a lack thereof. These documents then also create your historical file to review to help you determine the appropriate final ratings. Document all year long, not just the few weeks or days before the formal review.

5. Coach, re-align, and develop all year long.

Good managers monitor their employees' performance constantly to determine when and how they may need support. Performance that starts to veer off-track can be quickly refocused with a Necessary Conversation—and missing skills can be addressed through training or other means. Good managers are vigilant. They provide the guidance and tools needed to keep their employees focused and in constant growth and development mode.

6. Evaluate Job Performance.

This is finally the actual rating of the employee's performance for the official performance review. Unfortunately, many ineffective managers skip Steps 1-5 and then wonder why employees dread performance reviews! If good and not-so-good performance has been documented all year, the actual form completion is just a matter of pulling your documentation and recording the history that's been tracked—and discussed—all year long, and assigning the appropriate rating to the level of performance for each item that's being rated. The better you do Steps 1-5 above, the easier and more truthful evaluating job performance becomes.

7. Hold Performance Review Meetings.

Similarly, if you do steps 1-6 above, these meetings should be rather enjoyable and should hold no surprises about past performance. All issues concerning past performance will have been addressed in real-time. This official Performance Review Meeting then becomes a productive time to review the rating form—which again —should hold no surprises.

If you document and provide specific examples of the employee's performance over the full review period, the employee can assess for him or herself how his or her levels of performance align to those expected for "Exceptional" and the other ratings in each category rated. When you do this, there are fewer surprises and less need for explaining your ratings. Once the ratings have been discussed, you can then focus the bulk of your meeting time on discussing and developing goals and plans for the next year or upcoming rating period.

These goals and plans become a guide for both you and the employee. If you've done your job right, the performance review meeting becomes a quick recap of what's happened and has already been discussed, and then focuses on the future and the goals needed to work on and track over the upcoming review period.

8. Coach and communicate all year long.

By coaching and communicating all year long, you will build a solid, trusting relationship with your team. There will be no need to lie on performance reviews. You will have built the type of relationship with your team that immediately and honestly lets them know what's working and what's not. There will be no surprises. You'll be transparent. You'll be honest. You won't lie on performance reviews.

"The more accountable I can make you, the easier it is for you to show you're a great performer."

— *Mark V. Hurd, co-president and director, Oracle*

{ 6 } Stop Demanding More of Your Star Performers While Allowing Underperformers to Simply Show Up

"Management is the opportunity to help

people become better people. Practiced that

way, it's a magnificent profession."

— Clayton M. Christensen, Business

Administration professor, Harvard Business

School

WHY: YOU'LL TICK off your star performers in less time than you would believe.

I had lunch recently with Carol who is starting to hate her job. Carol drives to work Monday mornings dreading the day and by 10 AM, she's plotting her escape. By Wednesday noon, Carol looks forward to Friday and every Sunday evening Carol's anxiety level bubbles up because Monday's coming all too soon again.

The truly sad part of this story is that Carol's not a newly hired, uninformed employee. Carol's not a do-the-bare-minimum type of person. She's not a negative person with a victim's perspective of life. Carol's a successful, effective senior level manager and department head who has accomplished several high-profile, multi-million dollar projects. She's completed them on time, within budget and with minimal political fall-out. Then what is the problem? As Carol said it, "I love what I do. I just hate my job."

Hmmm, how can that be? Easy. The key responsibilities and tasks that are critical parts of Carol's job are challenging and wonderful learning opportunities. Her team is made up of smart dedicated professionals, and she's amassed a respected group of consultants and contractors to support her team's work. So what's the problem? Her manager—he doesn't seem to care that Carol makes things happen when no one else can. He provides her with little recognition, respect or acknowledgement for a job well done. Carol gets no additional compensation, bonus or merit awards. Carol's been told there is nothing she can do to earn an "Exceptional" on her performance review and that she'll get an "Acceptable" just like everyone else.

To top off her frustration, Carol shared:

"Because he knows I'm dedicated and I care about my reputation, I'll do the work until it's done and it's done right. So he dumps work on me and my department that clearly should be handled elsewhere. Because some of the other managers can't or don't deliver, he dumps the work on me. He says he's coaching them, but he's simply afraid to deal with them. So he spreads their work

around knowing my team and I and a few other departments will cover."

Put yourself in Carol's shoes. How would you feel if you gave your job your all: met deadlines, improved budget numbers, created strong professional networks and employee connections, only to be met with a half-hearted pat on the back? How would you feel if you believed you were expected to work harder than others—with no support or acknowledgement? I know I'd get sick of it pretty quickly and would want to work someplace else where I would be supported, appreciated, and respected. You'd probably feel the same way too.

Now, let's look at this situation from a larger leadership and organizational development perspective. Carol's manager is being incredibly foolish for not supporting and encouraging her more. She's been a star performer for years, has made and saved millions for the organization, and has been a key player in the organization attaining its industry-leadership position. Yet, he chooses to over-load and take Carol and her team for granted, while he completely ignores the poor performance of others, or he spends inordinate amounts of time trying to coach them back to "Acceptable" performance.

Now here's the key question: *If he succeeds and is able to re-focus these problem employees to be "Acceptable" again, what impact will they have on the organization?* Minimal. However, if he loses a star performer or fails to keep his star performers excited, creative and moving forward, what impact does that loss have on the organization? Serious...possibly deadly.

If you ignore or lose a star performer, what impact does that loss have on your organization?

Here's what I suggest you do instead: As a manager, you shouldn't ignore any employee. However, you can't spend equal amounts of time with all of them either. So focus your time and energies wisely and spend them where they'll have the most positive impact. Support your stars and help them identify ways to be even more successful. Address the problem employees and poor performers—don't condone their behavior by ignoring them. Finally, don't spend excessive amounts of time trying to coach employees who are not a "right fit" for the position or your organization. Know when it's time to say good-bye to them.

Spend time bringing your under-performers up to speed if you can, but don't ignore your stars in the process. Support them. Acknowledge them. Help them do and achieve even more. You may need to help unburden them, if you've unfairly over-loaded them. You'll also need to help unburden them, if they've done it to themselves.

When you've got a star or a few star employees who have done it all, been it all, and run it all for years, it's almost impossible to imagine anyone else being your go-to person. However, as an effective manager, you need to anticipate *what you are going to do* if and when that star employee leaves.

Russ was my client's star employee. Russ was their superman: Whenever an employee couldn't get the job done, Russ figured out how to do it and got it done himself. Because it was just quicker for Russ to do things himself, he did. Because of this, Russ had turned into a control-freak. He hadn't developed his team. He hadn't shared knowledge with others. He hadn't developed a back-up. He liked having all the knowledge and control. That way, no one could "mess anything up."

Yet Russ also complained about having to do everything himself. Russ complained about the situation he'd created himself. In talking with my client about Russ and the risky position he was putting their company in if anything should happen to Russ, I shared the following process to unburden Russ and spread the knowledge and work around to better leverage other team members, strengthen their talent pool, and relieve Russ of his heavy workload.

Steps to Analyze Workload and Distribute Tasks More Effectively:

1. Review the Workload: Review with Russ everything he does in the course of a day, a week, and a month. Then, just write it down in a basic list format. This first step alone may well make you tremble as you see first-hand everything Russ is involved in and responsible for doing. It will also shed light on just what Russ spends his time doing, that he shouldn't be doing. You'll no doubt discover that Russ spends a great deal of time doing basic tasks that his staff should be handling, but they don't because "Russ has always done it."

This exercise allows you to get a good look at what tasks Russ is doing that are appropriate for his position, and what tasks he is doing that should and could be handled by other staff. *(Note: You should also review the entire team's workload with Russ to help him realign and redistribute tasks and responsibilities appropriately.)*

2. Realign Tasks to the Appropriate Position: Given what you learn in Step 1, realign and redirect tasks to the most appropriate positions. Develop a training and career-development plan for all affected employees to phase-in the tasks that have been moved to them. Ensure your employees understand what timeline you're working on and when they need to have the "new" skills firmly in place to enable them to receive at least an "Acceptable" rating from you.

This transfer of knowledge from Russ to others is critical to not only your department but to others as well. Have your human resources and/or training manager work with you and Russ to develop basic training and "responsibility shift" plans and schedules to move tasks from Russ to others. *(Note: This is a skill Russ lacks and therefore hasn't done. You and your HR/*

Training professional need to walk him through the steps.)

3. Repeat with Other Key Staff: Repeat this process with other key staff first and then with all staff to determine how to best organize and fairly distribute their workloads.

4. Pay Attention: Pay attention to your staff day-in and day-out to determine more quickly when you've ignored them, over-burdened them, or allowed them to over-burden themselves. Nip those behaviors in the bud. Fairly distribute work. Hold all employees accountable and teach your well-meaning stars how to develop others.

As a manager, one of your responsibilities is to not only produce day-in and day-out, but to also develop a pool of skilled employees who are responsible and able to fulfill their current and future job responsibilities. To achieve that, you can't ask your stars to be and do it all. So don't. Don't take your shining stars for granted.

"It works that way with a lot of things in life. Once you're held accountable for something, you put in a lot more and make a more conscious effort."

— *Essence Carson, WNBA player, New York Liberty*

{ 7 } Stop Thinking a Bad Hire Will Change

"In the minds of great managers, consistent

poor performance is not primarily a matter of

weakness, stupidity, disobedience, or disrespect.

It is a matter of miscasting."

— *Marcus Buckingham, author, First,*

Break All the Rules: What the World's Greatest

Managers Do Differently

WHY: IF AN employee is not a good fit for your company, the employee will never be a good fit for your company. The employee should never have been hired. It's time to make a change and move on.

As the American Writer Paul Dickson said, "Never try to teach a pig to sing; it wastes your time and it annoys the pig." I know that's a crude analogy, but the point is: Don't try to force an employee to do something he or she isn't meant to do. Know when to stop trying to force a change and face reality: *This employee isn't going to change to become a good-fit employee here.* It's time to stop forcing the issue, make a change, and move on.

Know when it's time to stop forcing the issue, make a change, and move on.

After a strategic planning work session, Seth asked to speak with me. One of his field managers, Ronald, was frustrating him and the other managers. He'd been with the company 15 years and was a nice guy. Yet, while Seth had been on vacation, the other field managers didn't know where Ronald was half the time. As had been the case, Ronald's field crews performed fairly well, but they could've been more efficient. To top it all off, Seth had just found out Ronald intentionally changed data in a project file he'd been told to let another team member manage.

I asked if this behavior was new or if he'd seen Ronald do similar things before.

"Well, intentionally changing data is new, but I've always had problems with him. He's not organized. He doesn't keep his clients, team, or me updated. He doesn't return phone calls. He's not really capable of doing the job he has, that's why I hired Aaron. I've tried and tried over the years to help him, and he just doesn't step up to the plate. What else can I do?"

"You need to have a Necessary Conversation with Ronald and potentially start the official process towards termination."

"Oh I really don't want to do that."

We've all had this experience at least once in our professional lives: We've held off firing an employee because we didn't want to be mean or have that uncomfortable conversation. We didn't want to hire and train someone new who could be as bad or worse! We didn't want to disrupt the frustrating situation we had come to accept as normal. So, we didn't. We kept a poor performer on our payroll. Besides, it's better to have someone than no one, right?

Wrong! It's wrong and deep down we know it. We know it because we complain about them. We know it because we hear other employees complain about the poor performers. We know it because we've seen the barely acceptable work they produce. We know it because we spend more time focusing on them, their mistakes, and their disruptions than we spend coordinating activities with our strong, star employees. We know it because we spend our time doing their jobs instead of our own.

Disrupt the frustrating situations you have come to accept as normal!

In addition, we also have this nagging feeling that there's more going on than we realize. And, there usually is. It's the same old tip-of-the-iceberg adage. When we see an iceberg in the water, we only see the top, the tip. Any wise captain knows that the bulk of the iceberg is below the surface, unseen, and very much capable of ripping open a ship's hull and sinking the ship.

A problem employee's overt behaviors are typically only the tip of their performance issues. When we take the time to look deeper, a clearer picture of their limitations and dangers to our company become apparent. They may be the initial contact a customer has with our company—and they may be driving customers away. They may be in charge of our customer databases—and they may be allowing files to be corrupted and our future sales prospects stymied. They may be working with some of our most dedicated employees—and causing them frustration, irritation, and more work.

One of the best pieces of advice I received as a young manager was, "Sometimes you have to terminate an employee to 'force' her to find a job more suited to her personality, skills, and ambitions. If she's not happy here, be nice and 'help' her look for happiness someplace else." Does it make terminating an underperforming employee easy? No. Does it make terminating an employee who should have been terminated long ago or who should never have been hired easy? No. But it helps. And it's the right thing to do.

Here's what I suggest you do instead: Accept the fact that not every person is going to be a good-fit employee for your company. The person may be incredibly nice. The person may be trying to meet your performance standards. The person may have personal circumstances that are difficult. But the reality of the situation is still your reality: This person has not been, is not, and will not be a good fit for your team. This person's level of performance causes problems for you and other team members. Because of this, it's your responsibility to address this situation and resolve the problem.

Have the Necessary Conversations™. Give the employee a heads-up and a choice and a chance to perform to the standards required. Retrain and coach the employee. When he still can't or won't perform to the standards required, start the process your company has in place to document and address unacceptable performance. When that process is exhausted, start the termination process.[*]

If a person has not been, is not, and will not be a good fit for your team and causes problems for your team, it's your responsibility to address the situation and resolve the problem.

---

[*] This is a suggested process only. Please consult your legal counsel and refer to your company's policies and governmental laws concerning employee reprimands and terminations.

Seth called me two weeks later. Jack, his lead field manager, had just resigned. Jack told him, "I'm going back to my old company. They've offered me my old job back. I won't have to babysit another field manager there like I've had to babysit Ronald here. I'll be able to focus on my team and support the guys who *are* doing their jobs."

Seth said, *"Liz, I'm worried my other field manager may leave next! I'm losing my best people because I kept thinking I could change someone who's never been able to do the job I've been paying him to do. I can't lose any more good people by keeping someone I should have let go long ago."*

The next time you need to do your job as a manager, remember to be nice and fire an employee when it's the right thing to do. Don't spend excessive amounts of time trying to coach someone who isn't a good fit. Stop forcing the issue. Make a change and move on.

"It's not the people you fire who make your life miserable. It's the people you don't."

— Dick Grote, author, Discipline Without Punishment: The Proven Strategy That Turns Problem Employees Into Superior Performers

{ 8 } Stop Thinking That Telling is the Same as Teaching or Coaching

"What I hear, I forget. What I see, I remember. What I do, I understand."

— *Confucius*

WHY: MANY MANAGERS incorrectly believe that simply telling an employee how to do something constitutes training. Sorry it doesn't. Telling isn't teaching or coaching. Telling is giving a command or giving direction. Teaching or coaching is sharing knowledge and developing skills. If you want your team members to do something, tell them. If you want your team members to learn how to do something so they can perform competently on their own going forward, you need to spend time training and coaching them.

Telling isn't teaching or coaching.

Telling is giving a command or direction.

Teaching or coaching is sharing

knowledge and developing skills.

While attending a client's senior level meeting, several managers complained about the weak or under-developed personnel and project management skills in their direct-report managers. The really interesting thing was: Almost all of these senior managers are individuals who themselves had these same weak skills just a few short years ago. Huh. I wonder how they strengthened them?

It's no surprise: they developed them by being trained and coached. These managers were exposed to various situations that required them to employ personnel, interpersonal, and project management skills to some degree. They had to participate in and ultimately lead challenging projects. They had to coach and train others. They participated in training and coaching programs themselves, and they were held accountable by their managers, coaches, and others to learn, to try, and ultimately to "naturally" do many of the things effective managers and leaders do.

The key is: They were taught. They were coached. Someone or several others spent time on them and with them, sharing insights, tips, and lessons learned. Others cared enough about them and their futures to not just tell them what to do, but to teach them how to do it.

Tina was one of their direct-report managers and had been managing a virtual team for about ten months. Her virtual team was comprised of people she hadn't selected and hadn't worked with before. Her team was also comprised of people who didn't have her level of expertise. In addition, Tina's department had gone through a reorganization and workload shift.

As a result, Tina's manager was also forcing Tina to let go of numerous tasks and delegate them to her appropriate new team members. To do that, Tina had to not only redistribute work, but she had to train her team on how to do what she knew how to do so well. My initial coaching conversation with her went like this:

"It'd be so much easier if I could just do this myself. " Tina said as she looked at me with a mix of barely contained anger and frustration. *"I know you want me to delegate, but Kara is an idiot. She doesn't know what she's doing. She's wasted so*

much time trying to figure this stuff out. If she had just called me right away yesterday when she started having problems, I could have told her what to do. Instead, she wasted most of yesterday and this morning working on her own and it's still messed up. This isn't that difficult. I'm shocked at what she doesn't know. I just told her what to do again. I hope she doesn't make a bigger mess out of things."

"Is she learning and making progress or is she simply doing what you tell her?"

"I think she's learning. But honestly, this would be done by now if I'd have just done it myself."

"If you do it, how will she learn?"

"I know. I know. By teaching her, she'll learn and I don't have to do it myself. But man-o-man, this is painful!"

"Yeah well, that's why you have the sexy title of 'manager.' You get to train others. Now, here's the really painful part: It doesn't sound as if you've been training Kara. It sounds as if you've been giving her instructions. If you keep giving her instructions, she'll keep coming back for the next set of instructions when she completes the current set. If you train her, she'll learn to think ahead on her own."

"Ah crud!"

Here's what I suggest you do instead: Don't just tell employees what to do; teach and coach them why and how. And that takes time and focus.

One of the fundamental responsibilities in management is to develop the people for whom we are responsible. We're supposed to help them continuously develop enhanced or new skills to ensure they're capable of performing at a level our company will need them to perform 1, 2 or 3 years from now. And, we need to do this while meeting current production requirements, dealing with the operational issues that arise, addressing team and personnel issues, and hitting our sales and profitability numbers.

To add to the frustration, most managers aren't trained on how to train or coach others. Yet, more often than not, the most often studied trainer is you, the manager. You're the member of the leadership team most staff pay attention to every day. You're the one they model, take their cues from and develop their skills because of. You're it. So it's time to conscientiously analyze how you do what you do and segment it so others can learn in bite-sized pieces, just as you did. Your team members won't need to learn everything you learned or in the same order - because your organization is different now than it was when you learned select skills. However, your team members will need to learn many of the same skills you've struggled to master.

So here are a few pointers on training and coaching others:

Learning Styles: Just as people have differing dominant personality and communication styles, people have differing dominant learning styles. People learn in different ways and not everyone will just "get it" by being told what to do. The learning style that works best for you, may not work well for your team members.

There are **visual** learners who learn best when they can see something being done. Visual learners like to have others show them how to do things. They like demonstrations and videos. For many visual learners, if they can see how it's done, they can then more easily do it themselves.

Auditory learners learn best by hearing, listening to others, and reading. They learn when given instructions and when reading instructions. Auditory learners like webinars and listening to audio programs while they drive, exercise, work, or just relax.

Kinesthetic or **physical** learners learn best when they are able to physically engage and do the new skill or procedure themselves. They want to "get their hands on it and play with it to see how it works." Kinesthetic learners appreciate working with models, case studies, and relevant practice exercises.

Finally, just as we tend to speak to others in our preferred, dominant personality and communication style, we tend to teach others using our own preferred learning style. So visual learners, tend to use a lot of visuals, auditory learners tend to give instructions, and kinesthetic learners tend to create hands-on, practice scenarios. However, what works for you, may not be right for others. So you need to address all learning style preferences to enhance the learning opportunities for your team members. To do that, be intentional in how you train others.

If you keep giving instructions, your team will keep coming back for the next set of instructions when they complete the current set. If you train your team, they'll learn to think on their own.

Training Others: Over the years, I've developed and used this process for training clients and training staff. I call it:

T.E.R.P.S.™ for Training:

T - Tell them why it matters. (Tell your team member why this task/job is important and why it's important they do it the way you will show them.)

E - Explain how and demonstrate. (Explain the process or the steps to follow, and then show the team member how to do it.)

R - Repeat how. (Have the team member restate the steps you just followed.)

P - Practice. (Have the team member practice while you watch and coach them.)

S - Support. (Let the team member know where to find support once you leave.)

Here's the beauty of this simple process; it addresses all three learning styles. Auditory learners are being engaged right from the beginning as they hear about the task and why it matters. They then are further engaged as you explain the steps and how to do the task. Visual learners are engaged next as you demonstrate how to do the task. The adrenaline spikes for all three learning styles, when you get to 'R—Repeat How' because this is where they initially think, "Ah crud! I don't remember everything she said. I'm going to look like an idiot because I can't repeat all the steps!"

That's actually what you want to happen. You want them to experience an adrenaline rush to ratchet up their focus. All styles will pay a bit closer attention as you outline the steps with them once again. They'll now more intently think about the steps, visualize them, so they can repeat them to you. Then, the kinesthetic learners get to do what it is you want them to do when you get to the 'P—Practice' step. Finally, with 'S—Support,' all three styles will learn where to go or who to seek out if they need additional support once you leave. It's a simple process that works for teaching adults, no matter how they like to learn.

Coaching Others: Like a good sports coach, a manager who coaches his or her team members well not only cheers them on, but also hones in on specific skills each team member needs to enhance. Then the coach either works with the team member directly or enlists the aid of others to help the team member. The key to coaching is to teach others how to do the new skill themselves.

Your Role As a Coach:

Don't tell them what to do. Teach them how to know what to do.

Don't fix their problems for them. Teach them how to solve their own problems.

Don't be the go-between. Teach them how to assertively address their own interpersonal, team, client, vendor and other issues.

Don't allow them to wait for opportunities. Teach them to be proactive and forward-thinking.

Don't enable only tactical, short-term thinking. Teach them to anticipate the bigger picture impact and consequences of their decisions and actions.

After spending several days coaching Kara, Tina gave me an update:

"You know, now that I've spent time slowing down to train and coach Kara, I feel sorry for her. She's been completely over-whelmed by this project, and is so grateful for the time I spend with her. It's obvious no one has taken the time to teach her how to think through these types of issues

before. My hunch is, in the past when she'd run into an issue, her managers would just tell her what to do to give her enough information to inch forward without checking to see if she knew what she was doing.

Now, all I do is spend time with her, focus on calming her down, analyze the problems with her, and then talk through one or two logical solutions. To not intimidate her, I'll say things like, 'Well, I'd try _____ next because then I could see if ...' or 'What if we were to do....' She's got so much to learn, but we're making headway."

Because of this experience, Tina now understood why I had her take the time to train and coach Kara. Tina could get more work done herself—although it was initially painful and time-consuming—but with Kara doing what she could on her own, Tina could do work that required her experience and expertise. She was getting more done and Kara was learning. Win-win.

"I absolutely believe that people, unless coached, never reach their maximum capabilities."

— *Bob Nardelli, former CEO, Chrysler Corporation and Home Depot*

{ 9 } Stop Ignoring Your Ability to Influence Others, Wherever You Work

"Each day you are leading by example.

Whether you realize it or not or whether it's

positive or negative, you are influencing those

around you."

— *Rob Liano, bestselling author and*

success coach

WHY: YOU'RE THE manager. Your team is always watching you, noticing what you say, and taking cues from you. How you deal with them and others during the good, bad, and ugly times matters. You are a role model for them to either emulate or do the opposite of.

We influence others' perceptions of us and their behaviors by what we say and what we do. Hopefully, you've had the opportunity to experience a team member or members say, "I really like working with you" or "I'm staying here because of you." If that's happened, you've had a serious, positive impact on someone. If instead, you've heard team members say, "I'm leaving because of you," well, you've had an impact too— just the wrong kind. Positively or negatively, we, as managers, influence others.

Glenn manages a team of 65 technicians and other IT support personnel. His company is planning a complete reorganization over the next two years. Glenn shared with me:

"My team is frustrated and morale is lower than I've ever seen it. The senior leadership team either changes their minds every few weeks as to how the reorganization is going to impact my team, or they don't tell me anything. They keep saying they're being transparent, but they're not. No one trusts them anymore. I don't know what to do. My team is frustrated and I know some of them are concerned about their futures here. I can't tell them anything because I don't know anything. I wish I could do something, but I can't."

Oh contraire. As I shared with Glenn, there are two main reasons I disagreed with his last statement:

First, as the manager, you have an obligation to positively influence the work environment of your team.

Second, every person has the capability to make a difference and influence others, not just the C-suite executives or those in management.

As the manager, it's your job to ensure your team's work environment is as conducive to focusing and doing good work as it can be. Regardless of the inconsistencies and inefficiencies of your superiors and others, you have an obligation to try to create a positive zone of influence for your team to shelter them from the unnecessary turmoil created by others, while also keeping them informed and focused on moving forward. It's not easy to do, but it's your job. It's not your job to sit back and say, "Everyone else is behaving poorly, so I will too. I'll give up." You need to continue to say and do things that will help your team perform to the best of their capabilities, regardless of what others—who should know better—do or don't do.

Keep sharing information. Keep providing feedback. Keep training and coaching them. Keep doing what a good manager is supposed to do. It's not that difficult and it may be what you're already doing.

For example:

Without even realizing it, you influenced Rita. She was one of your employees in your first management role nine years ago. Rita was a single mom who was trying to make ends meet while creating a future for her kids and herself. By enrolling her in a "Future Managers" program, you took a risk on her when no one else had in years. You helped her regain her confidence, increased her skills, and helped her provide for her family. Rita now tries to pay-it-forward by coaching and helping others as you helped her.

You influenced Beth Ann. She was a new hire to the company and to your team three years ago. Beth Ann had to sit at a spare desk in your office for two weeks until the office space was adequately reconfigured to accommodate her. During those two weeks, Beth Ann literally worked next to you, heard the majority of your telephone conversations, listened as you discussed and analyzed project and client scenarios with other team members, observed you interact with both "easy" and "challenging" team members, and studied how you handled stressful situations face-to-face and remotely.

To this day, Beth Ann tells others it was the best two weeks of training she could have had. She studied you as you thought things through, interacted with people, and managed projects.

You also influenced Terry, Rod, and Greg. They've each worked with you for almost six years. They've each seen you interact with upper management during the good times and the bad. They've seen you stay consistent and not bend to the whims and emotional reactions of others. They've seen you defend your team to upper management, and they've experienced you lose your temper with them for messing up. They've seen you at your less-than-best, but they all see you as one of the most fair and honest managers they've ever worked with. They stay because of you.

As a manager, you have a great capability and responsibility to influence others. Doing your job in a way that shows others you respect them, influences them. Addressing challenging problems with and on behalf of your team members, influences them. Holding staff accountable in a fair, honest, transparent way, influences them. Pointing out the talent and potential in others, influences them. Doing the right thing, influences others.

Do you have a favorite restaurant because you like the people who work there, the way they treat you, and oh yeah, the food is good? Do you have certain, go-to people you seek out for information, help, and solutions because you know you can count on them, and you like them? Do you credit someone in your past for saying something to you or doing something for you that helped you? All of these are basic examples of one's ability to influence you and your actions. These people who may have influenced you aren't necessarily "senior" in their organizations. They are front-line wait staff, administrative and technical support team members, or possibly peers. Their ability to influence you is not determined solely by their position. It is also determined by their character. The same holds true for you. Your ability to influence others is not determined solely by your position, but by your character and your desire to influence others positively or negatively.

Your ability to influence others is not determined solely by your position, but by your character and your desire to influence others positively or negatively.

With these ideas in mind, I suggested to Glenn:

"Continue to ask senior management for specific, short updates. Then start to hold quick team huddles every day and share what news you have. Use this time to then segue into what you

need the entire team and various members to focus on that day to meet immediate needs and address those longer-term needs that are being confirmed. Regardless of the lack of consistent information you're getting from above, demonstrate for your team how you will try to be as consistent and transparent as possible. You won't bash upper management; you'll just model a different type of leadership. I think you'll be amazed at how much they'll appreciate it. "

He did and they did.

Here's what I suggest you do instead: Accept the reality, that regardless of your position within the management hierarchy, you are a role model and you do influence others, positively or negatively. You have an obligation to create a positive work environment for your team and to provide the information and support they need, as you can, to do their jobs well.

To gauge your influence on others, take this *Management Influence Self-Test*: Ask yourself, "How many times has someone said to me something like, "I'm working here because I want to work with you." Once, twice, several times, all of the time—never?

I hope you are able to say once, twice or hopefully several times. If you are, that's a strong commentary on your leadership skills. You've obviously had a positive, professional impact on at least one person. Those few words speak volumes about you and your management style. You're a leader they want to learn from, work with, and follow. They like being influenced by you.

On the other hand, if you've never had anyone tell you, "Because of you, I'm here too," the absence of those words may be telling you:

Because of your leadership—or lack thereof—they don't want to be a part of the organization any longer.

Because of your leadership, they feel underappreciated, used, or ignored.

Because of your leadership, they aren't clued in, feel lost and uninformed.

Because of your leadership, they aren't challenged to learn, grow, and enhance their skills.

Because of your leadership, they've lost respect for the organization and no longer want to be associated with it.

Because of your leadership, they'd rather not have a job than have to spend more time being influenced by you. Ouch.

Choose to be a positive role model for your team and remember the reality that you will be influencing them whether you intend to or not. So why not choose to influence them in a way that will cause them to say, *"Because of you, I'm a better person."*

"The best thing you can do is get good at

being you."

— *Fortune Cookie*

{ 10 } Stop Listening When Others Tell You to Just Accept That "This is the Way Things Are"

"The right thing to do and the hard thing to

do are usually the same."

— Steve Maraboli, author, Life, the Truth,

and Being Free

WHY: IF A SITUATION doesn't feel right, there's probably something wrong. It may be wrong legally, ethically, or morally. Regardless of how wrong it may be, because it feels wrong to you, it's crossed a line with you and your personal values. So either do something about it, or get out of that environment because its values don't match yours. Don't accept the "This is just the way things are" mantra of others who have become complacent when they're supposed to be leading. Don't allow yourself to become a complacent manager. You'll lose your self-respect and the respect of others.

Dierdra called me to tell me about her new job. She'd been in her new management role for three months and was enjoying the exposure to new issues, people, and challenges. However, she was also surprised at the limited support she received from upper management on personnel disciplinary actions and challenges to contractor billings she'd tried to initiate.

"When I ask them to support me and my actions, they tell me not to worry about them. Just let things be." Dierdra sighed in frustration, *"If I've heard it once, I've heard it 20 times: This is just the way things are. You're not going to be able to do anything about them, just accept them.' But I don't want to just accept these things. These employees should have been terminated years ago and these contractors should not be paid for work they haven't done!"*

Doing the right thing is often not the easy thing. It's often the thing that takes a good deal of thought, work, persistence, patience, thought, work, persistence, patience... Because of that, many don't and won't do the right thing. They'll do nothing instead. They'll allow a poor behavior to continue, an incorrect invoice to be approved, a padded expense report to move forward, or a false statement to be presented as true. They'd rather do nothing and claim ignorance, than do something and face resistance.

If a situation doesn't feel right, there's probably something wrong. It may be wrong legally, ethically, or morally. Regardless of how wrong it may be, because it feels wrong to you, it's crossed

a line with you and your personal values.

Think over your professional career and identify one situation that, if you could do it over again, you would do differently. Identify a situation that you don't believe you did enough to address the issue properly the first time. There was more you could and should have done. What was that situation? Visualize it.

Now, if you could do it over again, how would you handle the situation differently this time around?

More often than not, when I ask these questions to my leadership training participants, they'll share that if they could do the situation over again, they would take more assertive, straight-forward actions to address the issues. They wouldn't avoid them or just accept them. They would do something more. But at the time, they didn't, and now these managers still recall these unsettling scenarios.

When I ask each group, "Have you ever faced anything more challenging than the particular situation you're recalling?" they always nod their heads yes. Yet the participants still thought of the particular situation they did... because they didn't handle it well the first time. They had downplayed the situation. They had ignored it. They had accepted what others told them even though it violated their professional and personal values. They had been complacent as managers.

Dierdra, on the other hand, doesn't believe in the word complacent. As she told me:

"Liz, I don't care if I lose my job over these things. I'm going to do something about them. These folks don't know me that well yet, but you know me. I'm not about to put my name on anything that isn't correct and that I can't attest to honestly. Just because previous managers moved employees around instead of firing them, I won't. Just because these contractors have never had anyone reject their invoices and expense

reports before, tough. I'm here to do my job, and I'm going to do it. They may not like it, but I'm going to do my job; I don't care if they don't do theirs."

She did and two years later Dierdra received a commendation for her service.

Here's what I suggest you do instead: If your head and your gut tell you something is wrong and needs to be corrected, do something about it. If you can't do anything about the situation, leave. Get yourself out of an environment that doesn't align with your values and beliefs. Don't readily accept what others claim as insurmountable obstacles and "that's just the way it is," for the sake of having a job. Don't allow their complacency to become yours.

My company provides training to government employees frequently. In doing so, we often hear participants say, "You don't understand government. That's just how it is around here." I can honestly say, I do understand government. I've worked either in it or with the government my entire professional career. If you don't like working for the government, leave. If you do, then work to improve the environment you work in or move to a different position or to a different agency. Just don't stay, continue to complain, and say there's nothing you can do. By doing that, you're no different than everyone else and the environment you're complaining about!

If you don't want to leave your current employer because you'll never make the kind of money or have the benefits you have now, then stay—but don't complain about it anymore. You've made a choice. Either stay and work to improve the organization or leave. The choice is yours. But choose to act in a way that will allow you to sleep soundly at night and look forward to work the next day. Choose to act and do things that help your team move forward, that make positive changes, and that allow you to say, "I made a difference. I wasn't complacent."

Choose to act and do things that help

your team move forward, that make

positive changes, and that allow you to

say, "I made a difference. I wasn't

complacent."

Address problems head-on!

Address Underperforming Employees—
When you come face-to-face with an
underperforming employee, don't move them
elsewhere and make their poor performance
someone else's issue. Do what you need to do to
clarify expectations, have Necessary
Conversations™, and then if necessary, start the

formalized process to terminate the team member's employment. Will it take work? Yes. Will it be frustrating? Yes. Will it be easier to just ignore them? No. No because you'll know you should be addressing the team member's poor performance and so will your team. Just because other managers haven't done their jobs in the past, doesn't justify you not doing yours.

Create a team of Engaged People—Do what may not have been done in the past by their prior managers: Treat your team members as adults and with respect. Clarify their job responsibilities and your expectations of them. Provide them with consistent feedback—the good and the bad so corrections can be made while issues are small.

Identify ways to clear frustrations and roadblocks for them that are making their jobs more difficult. Listen to them. Help them improve. Help their environment to improve. Be willing to do the right thing.

After she received her service commendation, Dierdra updated me on her management journey:

"Liz it's really been a challenging two years. I've been called everything from 'The Terminator' to' The Moral Majority'—and that was by my boss! There were times I fully anticipated I'd be fired. Contractors were calling my boss and my boss's boss to complain about me. When I let my manager know I wasn't going to sign anything that wasn't correct and that I had the data to

prove what was correct and what was not correct,

he finally supported me. It's been rough, but I'm

making headway and I feel really good about that.

My team members appreciate it too."

How you choose to act, react, or not act to situations matters. So make a choice each day to manage and lead with intent. Do something. Do the assertive thing. Do the right thing.

"Do what you feel in your heart to be right—for

you'll be criticized anyway."

— Eleanor Roosevelt, former First Lady of the

United States

Conclusion

"As a leader, I am tough on myself and I raise the standard for everybody. However, I am very caring because I want people to excel at what they are doing so that they can aspire to be me in the future."

— Indra Nooyi, Chairman and CEO, PepsiCo

BEING A MANAGER is both a great opportunity and a great responsibility. As a manager, you have tremendous influence on those you manage (for better or for worse), and you are an indispensable piece of the puzzle that determines your organization's direction. It's a challenging position. Managers often tell me how difficult it is to provide the right feedback to the right people at the right time and in the right way. It is difficult and not everyone is an effective manager. However, from my experience, the best managers are those who are constantly scanning for tips, techniques, and ideas to help them improve. They seek insights to help them manage better, interact better, and support their team members better.

With that in mind, if you've recognized yourself in any of the previous ten chapters, I'm glad. That means that you can start making meaningful changes *today* that will have an enormous impact on your team. You just have to do it. Don't wait for the "right" time.

However, keep in mind that when you raise your expectations of yourself as a manager and those you have of your team, you and your team will make mistakes. Your team may not easily acclimate to the new you, to the new expectations, or to the new consequences, but that's where your resolve and focus come into play.

It's up to you to maintain your progress. It's easy to become complacent, but it's not right.

Thank you for taking on the responsibility to manage others. Now, ask yourself:

Is there anything that I need to stop doing?

Continue Your Leadership Journey

Available at WBSLLC.com/Store

SOMETHING NEEDS TO CHANGE AROUND HERE
The Five Stages to Leveraging Your Leadership

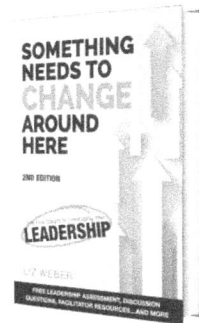

- Are you tired of working 50, 60, 70 or more hours a week?
- Are you frustrated by what your team members don't do and can't figure out for themselves?
- Do you come in early and stay late just so you can get things done?
- Would you like to get your life back?

IF YOU ANSWERED YES TO EVEN ONE OF THESE QUESTIONS, YOU NEED THIS BOOK!

If you walk around complaining about your team or muttering to yourself, "Something needs to change around here," you're right. And it's probably you.

DON'T LET 'EM TREAT YOU LIKE A GIRL® — A WOMAN'S GUIDE TO LEADERSHIP SUCCESS

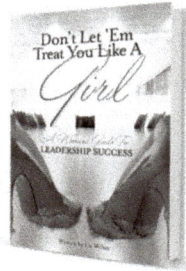

With insights gathered from women and men in leadership roles, Liz shares tips to help aspiring to experienced women leaders.

This quick-reading, insightful guide helps you identify:

- Which leadership traits are most admired
- What your leadership brand is saying about you
- How to manage conflicts and negotiations more effectively
- What "girly" behaviors you need to STOP!

This is a great resource for Women's Leadership programs!

Liz provides content-rich, interactive, skill-building presentations to groups large and small. Liz is known for her candor and her ability to customize her topics to meet your group's specific needs.

For more information, call +1(717)597.8890 or go to www.WBSLLC.com

About Liz Weber, CMC, CSP

In the words of one client, *"Liz Weber will help you see opportunities you never knew existed."*

Known for her candor, clear insights and straightforward approach, Liz Weber is a **sought-after management consultant, keynote speaker and seminar presenter**. She is one of fewer than 100 people in the U.S. to hold both the Certified Speaking Professional (CSP) and Certified Management Consultant (CMC) designations—the **highest earned designations in two different professions**.

As experts in strategic planning, succession planning and leadership development, Liz and her team are based near Harrisburg, Pennsylvania, and work with leaders to take their organizations:

- From no business strategy to enterprise-wide focus and clarity

- From no succession or workforce plan to enterprise-wide depth
- From a weak leadership team to a respected leadership team

Liz has supervised business activities in 129 countries and has consulted with organizations in over 20 countries. She has designed and facilitated conferences from Bangkok to Bonn and Tokyo to Tunis. Liz has taught for the Johns Hopkins University's Graduate School of Continuing Studies, as well as the Georgetown University's Senior Executive Leadership Program.

Liz is also the author of several leadership publications including:

- Something Needs to Change Around Here: The Five Stages to Leveraging Your Leadership
- Don't Let 'Em Treat You Like a Girl: A Woman's Guide to Leadership Success
- Stop So You Can Get The Results You Want

Liz's Manager's Corner column appears monthly in several trade publications, association newsletters, and internet resource centers for executives.